I FORGOT TO TELL YOU

Alton Douglas

To Lesley

Regards

Alton Douglas

BREWIN BOOKS

First published by
Brewin Books Ltd, 56 Alcester Road,
Studley, Warwickshire B80 7LG in 2008
www.brewinbooks.com

ISBN: 978-1-85858-433-1

A Cataloguing in Publication Record
for this title is available from the British Library.

Typeset in Galliard.
Printed in Great Britain by
Cromwell Press.

ACKNOWLEDGEMENTS

The main purpose of this book is to try to bring a smile to even the most tightly pursed lips because, although audiences might dispute it, I was a professional comedian for twenty years. The pursuit of laughter is a worthy enough objective, in itself but I could not resist including some of the strange coincidences and curious happenings that have peppered my life as a musician/comic/author. However, this is not a solo act. Nothing ever happens in total isolation and this collection is proof of that. So here is a heartfelt "Thank You" to:

TV producer/researcher, Keith Ackrill. Although we are pals and chat on a regular basis, he never seems to tire of my stream of anecdotes and he reminded me of so many that did not appear in my biography, "The Original Alton Douglas". So the fact that "I Forgot To Tell You" exists is mainly his fault.

John Clarke, the producer of over two dozen "joint-effort" BBC TV programmes, who became a friend in the process.

My nephew, Keith Price, who spends a great chunk of his life digging up the roots of our family tree.

Shirley Thompson, who survived the experience of working on my biography.

Fellow comedian, Andy "muscles-running-to-fat" Wade.

Ken Windsor, our webmaster and close friend.

Finally, Jo, who not only knocks my diabolical paperwork into shape but also my life as well.

Any errors are entirely the responsibility of the reader.

"REMEMBERING WHAT'S-HIS-NAME"

I rang Vivian Stanshall (of Bonzo Dog Doo Dah Band fame) at his home in Muswell Hill, sometime after our Summer Season with The Temperance Seven. The answering machine clicked on and I heard his unmistakable voice, with its customary perfect elocution, "IF YOU HAVE ANYTHING FILTHY TO SAY, PLEASE SPEAK CLEARLY AFTER THE TONE."

* * * *

Old habits die hard. I had known Mark "The International Pickpocket" Raffles for many years when Pete Lindup and I stopped to chat to him at ATV in Borehamwood. As we walked away I commented to Pete, "Nice chap and a brilliant act." Pete said, "Yes and did you know that all the while you were talking to him he took the opportunity to practise going through your pockets?"

* * * *

In the days when being breathalysed involved blowing into a transparent plastic bag, Trevor Little, the children's entertainer (speciality: balloon modelling) was stopped by the police, "Would you mind blowing into this, sir?" "Certainly. Would you like an elephant or a giraffe?"

* * * *

Walking along the BBC corridor, in Shepherds Bush, the weatherman, Jack Scott, came towards me. A man shouted out, "Jack, I'm going fishing to-morrow. What's the official weather forecast?" Without missing a beat he walked to the window, looked out for a second and said, "Looks as if it'll be fine to me."

The ventriloquist, Johnny Roberts, told me that he was on stage in the North East and a drunk kept heckling him. He eventually managed to squash him with a well chosen put-down, only for the man to yell, "I'll come up there and kill you in a minute." He pleaded, "Look mate, I'm only doing my job." The drunk shouted, "I'm not talking to you. I'm talking to the little bloke."

* * * *

That reminds me, I once found a report in the Club Herald which read, "The ventriloquist's act would have been greatly improved if he had put the dummy nearer to the microphone."

* * * *

The Club Herald – again – carried a report with this priceless gem, "The night was spoiled because two of the double act failed to turn up."

* * * *

Speaking of ventriloquists, I worked with a Canadian vent and on the first day of our season together he said to me, "I bet you a fiver I can feel all the dancers' breasts in the next five minutes." Naturally, I took the bet on. Taking out of its box the most lovable teddy bear you have ever seen, he called to the dancers, "Say hello to Teddy, girls." With squeals of delight they all rushed over and took it in turns to cuddle the doll – forgetting there was a man's hand inside.

* * * *

Ken Dodd, speaking from his home in Knotty Ash said, "I haven't seen you for a while but I always think of you as being tall and handsome. I bet you're a little fat man now with a baldy head and a ponytail."

* * * *

The organist in one club provided the worst backing I had ever had in my life. After my act I stormed over to the entertainment secretary to give him a piece of my mind. Before I could speak he said, "I know, I know, everybody says the same thing. Where did we get him from? Well, I can tell you it costs us a pretty penny to get somebody as good as him."

At a club, deep in the Welsh valleys, the accompanist was a blind organist. Knowing of the miraculous powers that the visually-impaired sometimes possess I was impressed when I described my musical requirements to him. As I got to certain points, he would tap on the palm of his hand once or twice with the bowl of his upturned briar pipe. Later, after the most diabolical backing, I said to the drummer, "What were those signals he seemed to be giving himself? I thought he was trying to embed a thought in his subconscious, when he tapped on his palm with his pipe." The drummer scratched his head, "Oh, that – he was trying to get the burnt tobacco out of the bowl."

The one thing I was always complimented on, as a comedian, was my timing. However, one of the Torquay papers disagreed and said that I could learn a lot from adopting the technique of the one-man band on the same bill. When I tell you that he punctuated his gags by giving a double beat on the bass drum strapped to his back and by crashing the cymbals between his knees, I leave the rest to your judgement.

It was said of the agent, Billy Marsh, a chain-smoker, that he had stipulated in his will that he wished to be cremated and his ashes scattered over his suit.

* * * *

One summer I appeared at Weston-super-Mare with Tony Mercer (star of The Black and White Minstrel Show). He used to say, in the finale, "Some people assume that everyone in showbiz is gay. Well, I want to state here and now that I am not gay." Then, after a suitable pause, he would turn, point at me and say, "But if ever I change my mind, he'll be the first."

* * * *

People in showbiz, no matter how much acclaim they receive over the years, always seem to remember a snub – even an imagined one. I was signing books, at RAF Cosford, when a man came up and muttered, "Hello, Alton, I bet you don't remember me?" I replied, "I do. You're Norman Dodd, the singer and you came to see our show at Blackpool and walked out halfway through my act. I've smarted about that ever since." He gulped, "I've felt guilty about that for twenty years. I've always wanted to explain to you. You were running late and if I hadn't got back to the digs for eleven I'd have missed my supper."

* * * *

You know how, even in the noisiest of rooms, there can be a moment when everyone seems to stop talking at the same time? In the Green Room at ATV, one Sunday afternoon, in such a moment the publicist, George Bartram, turned to Ken Dodd and casually remarked, "Well, Ken, it's a long time since you and I had social intercourse." Everyone misheard him.

* * * *

George had quite a life as a showbiz publicist and his clients ranged from the film star, Alan Ladd, to Morecambe and Wise; from impressionist, Mike Yarwood, to The Ophthalmic Council of Great Britain; to even, at one time, me. He was not too good at prophecies though and when I described my forthcoming BBC TV series, "Know Your Place," to him he shook his head sadly. It ran for 3 years and regularly attracted over 2.5 million viewers, an unheard-of figure for a local programme. Although he was not a careless person, by nature, he did confess that he had mislaid a pen and ink drawing of Ken Dodd by John Lennon, along with the autographs of all four Beatles. (He had a large autograph collection and the only person who had refused him was Sir Winston Churchill.)

❋   ❋   ❋   ❋

Once, in an attempt to drum up interest from the papers, he arranged a date for one of his clients with a former Miss World. The assignment was so successful that they found themselves in bed together. In the middle of their nocturnal grapplings, George's client stopped, rolled off and had hysterics. The non-recipient of his amorous wooings said worriedly, "For God's sake, what's the matter?" "Nothing, I was just thinking what a fabulous publicist George Bartram is."

❋   ❋   ❋   ❋

At the height of Vince Hill's popularity the chairman of a large company contacted George and requested a major star to promote their products. George said, "What about Vince Hill?" The chairman, in all seriousness, replied, "I don't care where you shoot it. Who are you going to get as the star?"

❋   ❋   ❋   ❋

In 1975 I was booked by Hugh Charles as Principal Comic with the "Fol de Rols". Hugh had made his money mainly through his song-writing abilities ("There'll Always Be An England", "We'll Meet Again", etc.) but he told me that in the fifties he had staged one of the most lavish summer shows ever seen in Blackpool. It had two dozen dancing girls, wonderful sets and costumes and cost a staggering £50,000. He stood at the back of the stalls, on the opening night and watched as the audience filed out. Finding the suspense almost unbearable, he grabbed what looked like a typical middle-aged Northern couple, "Did you enjoy the show?" The husband stared hard at him, thought for a moment and then replied, "It were fancy."

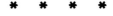

The comedian, Jimmy Wheeler (catchphrase: "Aye, aye, that's yer lot.") had, to put it mildly, a bit of a drink problem. After years of working the Butlins' circuit he arrived in Skegness to be told that if he appeared intoxicated, just one more time, that would be it. Well, that Sunday every pro in the town, who was not working, turned up to see how the drama developed. The curtains opened, the band played and on came a way over-the-eight Jimmy Wheeler. We all watched with horror as he staggered down to the footlights, tripped over and fell headfirst into the orchestra pit. There was a tremendous crash of cymbals, a long silence and then one hand came up and grasped the rail and then a second and finally Jimmy's head with, miraculously, his trilby hat still in place. Before he collapsed backwards, with an almighty wallop, we heard, "Aye, aye, Wheeler, that's yer lot."

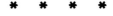

A comic was onstage, in a working men's club, getting bigger laughs than he had ever got in his life. Without the slightest effort the weakest gags in his act were getting roars. Just as he had got to the point where comics think they have reached the ultimate, he heard a commotion to his left and saw an old lady being helped on to the stage. He stopped, in mid-joke and said, "What is it, love?" As she got nearer he could see tears trickling down her cheeks and realised that she was almost helpless with laughter. Believing that he had found the dream fan, he moved towards her only to hear her gasp, "I just can't stand it any longer" and with that she reached down and tugged up his fly zip.

* * * *

One of my favourite characters was the veteran comic, Harold Berens. Chatting about unusual acts I mentioned the most famous whistler in the business. Harold said, "Ronnie Ronalde? I knew him before he had teeth!"

Harold was talking about his brief stay, as a comic, at the Windmill. Being one of the few venues where naked flesh could be seen, when anyone left the front rows there would be a terrific scramble over the seats to get the best positions. Viewing this Grand National spectacle, one afternoon, he could not resist, "Fellas, fellas, please – I know I'm attractive but this is ridiculous!"

* * * *

In my early days, as a comedian, I realised that I was totally unsuitable for stag shows. As I left one I heard, "I've seen some great comics – that wasn't one of 'em."

* * * *

During the pantomime run of "Goody Two Shoes", in Billingham, the local showbiz padre invited the principals to supper at the vicarage. Along with Helen Shapiro, Tom Mennard and Sandy Lane we were entertained and the wine and brandy flowed freely. My fondest image is of Macdonald Hobley and me standing in the doorway, in the early hours, waving goodbye to the vicar as he stumbled out through the front gate of his own home.

* * * *

On the subject of drink – we have a resident drunk in our neighbourhood who only surfaces, in daylight, about four times a year. On one of these rare occasions he staggered towards me:

Drunk "What time is it?"

A.D. "It's eight o'clock."

Drunk "No, I mean what time of the week is it?"

A.D. "It's Sunday morning."

Drunk "Aagh! I'll be late for f...... church."

* * * *

When I was working in the West End a sign in my hotel room read: "Will gentlemen please refrain from leaning their heads against the wall." What images that conjures up!

* * * *

One of my Blackpool landladies was the reincarnation of Mrs Malaprop. This will give you some idea: "I heard you last night riveting your engine" and when Dave Dee, Beaky, Mick and Tich were in town, "I hear Dave Dee's leaving Mairzy Doats." After hearing a radio programme about hermaphrodites she casually remarked, "I didn't know about them mufftites."

* * * *

Andy Wade enjoys telling this story against himself. After a terrible reception from an audience, one night, he came to the end of his act and thought, "Right, I'm not walking off without giving them what for." He snarled, "When I leave here, I shall light up a cigar, pull my fur collar round my neck, climb into my Porsche and drive off to my detached bungalow in the country." A bloke at the back yelled, "Blimey, your wife must have a good job."

* * * *

Jo and I do not accept too many party invitations because when people know that you have been involved in humour they either expect you to be permanently 'on' or to at least extend an ear to their joke telling. Another hazard is the chap who must impress on you that his wife could have been a really famous singer if she had persevered with her career. At one such event I was cornered by a man whose wife would have made all other girl singers sound like Louis Armstrong. He smirked, "And many's the time I've sat at the back of the theatre and listened to her glorious voice." I could not resist it any longer, "I can't understand that," I responded, "If she's so good why didn't you sit at the front?"

* * * *

Before I learned my lesson, I was appearing in the West End when the double act, Hinge and Bracket, invited me to a party. I remarked, purely in jest, "I'll come, have a drink thrown over me and leave." As I walked in someone asked, "Have you met Richard O'Sullivan?" The actor stretched out his hand, forgetting he was holding a drink. Exit.

* * * *

Standing at the stage door, at the Birmingham Hippodrome, as the American singer, Billy Eckstine, was signing autographs, I heard a girl squeal, "Ooh, I couldn't have got any closer to him!" Her friend countered, "You could have!!"

* * * *

I came out of the stage door at Barnsley Civic Hall with gravel-voiced singer, Tommy Bruce ("Ain't Misbehavin' ", etc.) and we were confronted with just three girls. Tommy turned to me, "I can remember when there used to be hundreds of screaming women waiting for me," he growled and then, brightening up, "But these three are better looking."

* * * *

Leaving Malvern's Festival Theatre a girl asked Tom O'Connor for his autograph. As an afterthought she said to me, "I suppose I'd better have yours as well." Feeling rather disgruntled I muttered, "I shouldn't bother, I'm not a star." She said, "I know that – I've just seen your act."

* * * *

Another occasion, after a particularly good reception from the audience, at The Bachelors Show, at the New Theatre in Hull, I was signing merrily away and a girl said politely, "I did enjoy your act – did you learn it yourself?"

* * * *

I love the American comedian, Shecky Greene's story about the night Frank Sinatra saved his life. As Shecky came out of a nightclub five men leapt on him, beat him to the ground and were knocking seven bells out of him when Frank stepped out of the shadows and said quietly, "OK, fellas – that's enough."

* * * *

I worked, on several television programmes with the producer, John Clarke, and he told me this tale. It is so good that I have left it in his own words.

"I did a two-part documentary about a club show. It was called, "Have Show Will Travel" and was filmed over four successive nights as the show travelled to working men's clubs in Birmingham, Coventry, Wrexham and somewhere else now forgotten. As we finished the filming in Coventry and were wrapping, rolling up cables, packing away lamps, folding up cameras, a drunk staggered through the crowd of audience still slowly dispersing and said to me, "You from the BBC?" "I am," I replied. "You know what you want to do?" I flinched, expecting the usual well-informed and incisive criticism, "No, what?" "You want to get your cameras, and bring them here and film this show." He gestured grandly towards the stage. "But – that's what we have been doing, all evening." The drunk juddered to a standstill. He opened and shut his mouth once or twice and gazed around at the equipment and lights, "Never mind all that," he firmly stated. "You want to do as I say." So I did."

＊　　＊　　＊　　＊

A board on a grassy area in Birmingham read, "Do not park on this reservation" and some wit had chalked underneath, "As it upsets the Injuns."

＊　　＊　　＊　　＊

A neighbour told me that when he was out at work his son broke a kitchen window. His wife decided, instead of telling tales, to measure it up. She then went out to buy a piece of glass. When he got home she was in tears because it was far too small to fit the gap. He asked what she had used to size it up and she replied, not having a tape measure, she had used a piece of elastic.

＊　　＊　　＊　　＊

To go back a while – "The Glenn Miller Story" was showing at The West End cinema and I thought I would catch a matinee showing. By chance I had a trombone lesson that same night so I asked the manager if I could leave my instrument in his office. As I came out afterwards and walked along the corridor to retrieve it I heard him say to an usherette, "Has Glenn Miller been in for his trombone yet?"

*   *   *   *

Shortly after I was discharged from the Army I thought it might be a good idea if I taught myself the rudiments of double-bass playing. At a dance, one night, there was a party of musicians in from the string section of the City of Birmingham Symphony Orchestra. They spent the entire evening staring in open-mouthed disbelief at the wholly inept performance of one of the band. Relieved that there were no members of the brass section present he played a high percentage of numbers on trombone that night.

*   *   *   *

In the early days our quartet shared a platform with the mighty Graham Dalley Orchestra. Both bands were set up on stage and took it in hourly turns to play. My drummer reported back that one of their musicians had just said, in a voice full of incredulity, "Have you *heard* that lot down the rough end?"

*   *   *   *

When one of my musicians was on holiday I booked a dep trumpet player for an afternoon wedding. He asked, as he had to come straight from work, if I would mind if he came in the firm's van. I admit to being a bit surprised when he turned up in a refrigerated meat wagon with the carcasses still inside.

*   *   *   *

There is nothing like getting off on the wrong foot! All my life I have had the childish habit of taking the mickey out of people's names so when my soon-to-be publisher, Alan Brewin, came to see me about our first book together, I was determined to be on my best behaviour. As he came up the path I kept repeating the mantra, "Don't take the mickey, don't take the mickey ...." The doorbell rang, I opened the door and said, "Come on in Alan, coffee's brewin'."

✳   ✳   ✳   ✳

A girl who worked in an office, in the centre of Birmingham, told Jo this story. The receptionist walked into the typing pool and said, "Karen, there's a man downstairs to see you." Karen was puzzled, "Someone for me? What does he look like?" The girl replied, "Well, his head's completely shaven on both sides and he's got a comb of hair in the middle, dyed orange. He's got a ring through his left nostril and one in each ear, he's all in black, with very short trousers, no socks and big boots. He's got tattoos all over his hands and arms and silver studs absolutely everywhere." Karen thought for a moment, "I've no idea who it is – that could be anybody."

✳   ✳   ✳   ✳

It must have been the same lad who boarded a bus and the driver said, "It'll be a pound for you and 50p for your parrot."

✳   ✳   ✳   ✳

Knowing I loved Jewish humour, Bertie Green, who owned the Astor Club, in London, told me about a friend of his. Apparently he took a girl for a ride in a taxi and she was so beautiful he could hardly keep his eyes on the meter.

✳   ✳   ✳   ✳

"BY COINCIDENCE..."

Just after the war Dad decided to surprise Mum and buy a car. I should mention that being a Dorothy, she was addressed by quite a lot of the family as Dolly (a name she hated). Now, in those days, remember, you could not choose your registration number. Anyway, he bought it and drove it home. As he parked the car outside he realised that the registration plate read DOL 161.

He begged her not to look around at the offside. Somebody had hit it on the way home.

*   *   *   *

The only car accident I was involved in, during the short period when I worked as a part-time insurance agent, happened well away from my work area when I ran into one of my own policyholders.

*   *   *   *

Amongst Jo's teachers, at the British School of Commerce, in the late forties was a Mr Bates. Roll back the years to 1908 and we find her dad, at Five Ways Grammar School, being taught by the same teacher.

*   *   *   *

"A Lawn for Spindlethrift", my one and only attempt at writing a one-act play, won first prize in the Illyrian Theatre's Playwriting Competition and the Tamworth Drama Festival. Encouraged by this, I opened the Writers' and Artists' Yearbook and used a pin to pick a Literary Agent. It selected Peter Crouch Associates in London. I posted it off and the following week I received a reply, written by Sheila Lemon – who had been in the same year as me at Saltley Grammar School.

*   *   *   *

Riding along the Coventry Road on my Vespa scooter I saw an elderly lady about two-thirds of the way across and went to pass behind her. She obviously changed her mind, turned and walked straight into me. Fortunately, she was not badly hurt and I finished up with an excellent witness who was able to explain that I was not to blame. I had sailed through the air and landed at the feet of a sergeant standing on the steps of Hay Mills Police Station – the very police station where Dad had served, throughout the war, as a Special Constable.

A contact put me in touch with a man called Fred Dorrell. He had worked at Castle Bromwich Aeroplane Factory, along with thousands of people involved in war production. Fred had a collection of photographs that he was prepared to loan me for my book, "Birmingham at War Volume 2". One picture he did not offer me was propped up on top of his television set and being nosey, that was the one I most wanted to see. "Oh, it's only a group of us standing by a Spitfire." "Just let me have a look, Fred – this really does interest me – that's my dad standing there." "Sidney was your dad? He was my best friend."

Immediately after the war Dad was hired, as a detective, to eliminate a spate of thefts at several Butlins' Holiday Camps, which he did with great success. Thirty years later, as a comic I did a tour of the same sites. With slightly less success.

Dad's favourite film was, "They Died With Their Boots On", starring Errol Flynn. Ten years or so after he died I was contacted by a man called Pat Collier Ryan who thought I might like to write the libretto for a planned musical called, "Usnah" (set in Ireland and involving the Little People). We agreed to meet in a café in Soho and he asked me if I would mind if he brought a friend along. I should explain that Pat was a professional film cameraman, currently working for the cinema, on a number of films in the "Look At Life" series. He brought with him the man who was recording the voiceover for the haunted houses sequence – a heavily bloated and very drunk Errol Flynn.

The name Dolly crops up again but this time it was an aunt of Jo's. Not having a television set she would often spend the evening with Jo's parents and in the mid 50's they were watching the programme, "1984". She was absolutely terrified and asked to be taken home. For several years after that she referred to it as the most horrific thing she had ever seen. She died, 30 years later, in 1984.

One of my music teachers was the fine trombonist, Fred Mercer. Fifty years later a friend of mine, involved in a house clearance, realised that the deceased was Fred. Looking through his belongings he discovered that he had bought almost every one of our books on Birmingham. He also found the manuscript for a song we had written together called "Rocking That Road to Nowhere".

Olive Pocius wrote to me from Florida. She had looked after me when I was a child and we had re-established our relationship in recent years. Now, she was excited to tell me that, after sending a copy of my biography to her brother, Robin, she had just had a surprising conversation with him. In the book I had mentioned that my favourite cowboy star was Randolph Scott and Robin told her that his friend, a fellow-Episcopalian priest, in the next parish in Scotland, was absolutely thrilled. She had asked him why and he replied, "Because he's Christopher Scott – Randolph's son!"

(Randolph Scott appeared in over 60 Westerns.)

*   *   *   *

Although my cousin, Pete Lucas and I did not even know of each others' existence, we had not only lived less than a mile apart but both of us had spent several years as professional comedians.

*   *   *   *

Jo and I decided, at short notice, to get married on 26th September 1970. When we arrived home we discovered that it was not only the same date as my parent's marriage but it was exactly 50 years to the day. Also, like us, dreading any form of pomp or ceremony, they had chosen a register office with just the necessary witnesses present.

*   *   *   *

When my mother died, in 1973, as part of the house clearance we gave away a lot of my old books, including a dictionary from my school days. Twenty-five years later a friend, rummaging around at a car boot sale, bought it for 50p. It is now back in my bookcase.

*   *   *   *

Jo and I have lived at three addresses, over the years, with the numbers 371, 218 and 290. Each set of digits adds up to 11. Also, her birthday is on the 1st and mine the 22nd. Is it any wonder that our lucky number is - - - guess?

*   *   *   *

In my teens my great passion was cricket and my bowling hero was the Warwickshire spinner, Eric Hollies (he was virtually 'infamous' for having bowled Don Bradman out for a duck in his last Test innings). Jo, discussing her schooldays remarked, "I was in the same class as a famous cricketer's daughter." "Oh, yes. Who was that?" "Jackie Hollies."

*   *   *   *

Cyril Sprenger, the jazz pianist and I were chatting one night and I told him that as a Patron of The Birmingham Tapes for the Handicapped I had spent part of the day recording my Christmas message. As a regular feature, each year I would do my impression of Max Wall and then Max, another of the Patrons, would record his reply. (Max Wall voice) "I've 'eard it. You'll have young Freddie Starr after you!" Cyril said, "Next time you speak to Max, give him my regards. He was my Drill Instructor in the RAF in Blackpool." (In those days Max was Corporal Lorimer.)

*   *   *   *

Johnny Dawson, the oboe player I shared a room with at Catterick, in my National Service days, eventually became the Bandmaster of the Green Howards, the regiment in which my publisher, Alan Brewin, served. (Incidentally, Johnny, who was a life-long Socialist, went on to become the Steward of Richmond Conservative Club.)

*   *   *   *

As a lad the first two 78rpm records I bought were Eddie Calvert's, "Oh Mein Papa" and Winifred Atwell's, "Black and White Rag". The first name we ever worked with, as a band, was Eddie Calvert (at the Golden Butterfly Nightclub in Skegness) and one of the very first stars I appeared in cabaret with was Winifred Atwell (The Penguin Club in Birmingham).

✳　✳　✳　✳

Almost every year, when I was young, we would go to Weston-super-Mare for our holidays (because of its close proximity to Birmingham it was much favoured by Brummies and was christened, "Brum-by-the-Sea"). Never in my wildest dreams would I have imagined that I would get married there; appear in a summer season at the Knightstone Theatre; be chosen as the act for the opening week at the Glengarry Hotel and perform literally dozens of one-nighters in the town.

One of the dates was at the Webbington Country Club. The previous week the top of the bill had been one of the most glamorous film stars in the world – Jayne Mansfield. Because of her fee the budget for the rest of the show was minuscule. Part of her act involved a comedy sketch but the management could not afford to hire another actress so they used the cloakroom attendant.

✳　✳　✳　✳

Jane Fyffe and I were the acts booked, for a Sunday concert at Kings Heath Transport Club (not, at that time, the most glamorous of venues). The following morning we were both off to work in London. I was due to start a season at the Bestcellar nightclub, in Leicester Square and Jane was rehearsing for the West End musical, "Robert and Elizabeth", at the Lyric Theatre, opposite Keith Michel.

✳　✳　✳　✳

The week after I appeared at the Torbay Cabaret Club I was booked for a week at Birmingham's Monte Carlo Club. On the second night I received a call telling me that the Paignton venue had just had its front door fire-bombed. Two nights later the Monte Carlo lost its front door. Do not read anything into the fact that I seem to be the only common denominator.

A few weeks before Shirley Thompson had completed, "The Original Alton Douglas", I had a letter from a Mr Birt. He had bought one of our Birmingham books and spotted the name of Douglas Price in the Acknowledgements. He wanted to contact him although they had not spoken for over 50 years. I explained that it was actually my original name and it was included because we had used quite a lot of photographs from my personal collection and indeed, he and I had been friends as children.

What he did not know was that Shirley had spent the previous day ringing all the Birts she could trace to try and contact either him or his brother Roy.

Apart from the pleasure of talking to him again, he turned out to be an excellent interviewee and gave a whole new dimension to the section about my early life.

It must be in the genes. As well as the 40-plus books I have been involved in, my uncle, Victor J Price, was also the author of several titles ("Tracing Your Family Tree", "The Bull Ring", "Old Ladywood Remembered", etc.).

Touring the country I met and chatted on several occasions with Johnny Caesar (another comedian). It was not until years later that I found out, through our Regimental magazine, that he had also served in the 5th Royal Inniskilling Dragoon Guards (albeit at a different time to me) and although we had played in the band, neither of us had been officially recognised as bandsmen. (In my case because I was a National Serviceman and it would have meant paying me more money.)

* * * *

Purely by accident I seem to have had a series of musical healers. At Andy Waghmare's dental practice if you had the first appointment you would often have to wait whilst he finished his latest piano piece. When I had neck problems my first physiotherapist was Keith Hallam who played tenor sax (his colleague, Dai, across the corridor was a trombonist.) My current physio, Barry Maddox, frequently finishes his lunchtime practice session and opens the door still wearing his sax sling around his neck.

* * * *

Without my knowledge, the one-time pianist with my band, Alan Lewis, had successfully published two books of limericks. Out of the blue he wrote congratulating me after reading in a trade paper that my second book of children's nonsense verse had just appeared – including quite a few limericks.

* * * *

The week before I opened my summer season as Principal Comedian with the "Fol de Rols," in 1975, I appeared on Eammon Andrews' "Tonight" TV programme. Purely by chance, one of the other guests was Arthur Askey – the Fols' Principal Comedian in the thirties.

* * * *

I mention, in my biography, how I was sometimes mistaken for the actor, Anton Rodgers and I admit that there is something of a resemblance. Anyway, I arrived to appear in cabaret, at March in Cambridgeshire and the anxious looking organiser said to me, "I should warn you that there's a lot of antagonism towards you. They know you were born down the road in Wisbech and they haven't forgiven you for not turning up to open the new hall last year." I explained to him that I was a Brummie through and through and that they must be thinking of Anton Rodgers. After a great deal of verbal jousting I eventually persuaded him. He then went out to introduce me and spent several minutes explaining that I was another bloke altogether, I came from the Midlands and they were to give me a chance. You try making a frustrated audience laugh when they have come out determined to hang you from the nearest lamppost.

✻ ✻ ✻ ✻

Coincidences do occur in literature too. I am sure that the American author, Ken Lord, has never heard of me and yet his book, "Requiem For a Character Actor", contains three of these. First of all the title; for a period of my show-business career I was classified as "a character actor" (appearing in several TV and radio dramas/comedies). Secondly, the Police Chief's name is Quentin Price and my family name is Price. Thirdly, one of the principals in the story is MAJOR ALTON DOUGLAS.

✻ ✻ ✻ ✻

"THE OLD CURIOSITY CROP"

One of the greatest surprises of my life came in the form of a letter from my old school, Saltley Grammar School (by then Saltley School). To go back – I had been a total duffer, failing at almost every aspect of scholastic achievement and languishing at the bottom of the lowest form, in my year, all through my six years. My sporting successes had been non-existent, indeed, a perfect match for my intellectual efforts. Therefore, it came as quite a shock when I received a letter telling me that they were putting together a gallery of successful former pupils (including Robert Kilroy–Silk) and intended hanging a blow-up photograph of me (in my role as an author) in the foyer. I can think of at least a couple of teachers who would have preferred to have hung me instead.

Our next door neighbour, in Small Heath, was a man called George Gould. He had served in the Royal Army Ordnance Corps, during the Second World War, been captured after the fall of Singapore and spent over 2 years as a prisoner of war in Thailand. During transportation to Japan his boat was hit by an American torpedo and out of 1,300 prisoners he was one of only 58 British survivors.

In the early fifties he offered to help me clear out one of our bedrooms. Under a pile of bric-a-brac we unearthed, to George's horror, a Japanese flag.

This story could have appeared in our chapter of coincidences but for me the most startling thing about this is why we should have possessed the flag in the first place?

(Some of George's wartime experiences were woven into the film script of "Return From The River Kwai".)

To commemorate the 1953 Coronation it was decided that Heather Road would not be left behind in the celebrations. Because it was quite a long road the committee then split it into two halves. By sheer chance our house was exactly bang in the middle. When the plans had been finalised someone noticed that we had been left out. We then received an invitation from both sections to join them. Mum took part in a coin-tossing ceremony and the top half won.

*　*　*　*

Frantic banging on the front door alerted us to a problem. A neighbour in floods of tears, "Can you help? The bailiffs are here and they are trying to repossess my furniture." I knew that she had a drink problem and it turned out that the money, intended to pay bills, had been used to quench her thirst. I asked the bailiff if I could look at the inventory on his clipboard. "Brown suite? Blue carpet? But looking through the window I can see a green suite and brown carpet? The man who compiled this list must have been colour-blind. You'll have to re-jig the inventory and come back again." The woman was delighted with the stay of execution and within two days managed to scrape the necessary funds together. Fast forward six months and I am chatting to a spiritualist friend of ours, Frances Glazebrook. She said, "Have you lost a car?" I said, "Yes, we had it stolen from the drive." "And have you helped a neighbour out recently?" So, I told her about the bailiff incident. She shook her head, "Well, I hate to tell you this but she was so desperate for money, about six months ago she organised the theft of your car."

Beacon Radio had sponsored the Herb Miller Orchestra at Dudley Town Hall. Because everyone at the station was totally immersed in rock music and I presented their big band programme, "Beacon Swing", I was the natural choice to act as their representative. I took my friend, Dennis Moore, with me and after the show he was thrilled to tell Herb, "During the war I heard your brother Glenn's orchestra playing in the grounds of Coventry Cathedral. When they'd finished he marched past me as close as I am to you." To our great surprise Herb responded, with quite obvious venom, "You should have stuck your foot out and tripped the bastard up."

＊　＊　＊　＊

Arnold Price was driving along New Street in his Rolls Royce, sometime in 1979. Slowing down outside Hudson's bookshop, he heard his back door open, somebody was bundled in and a male voice yelled, "Go!!!" He accelerated as quickly as he could, driving round the corner into Stephenson Place and screeched to a halt. He turned round and was flabbergasted to find himself gazing into the eyes of the film star, Sophia Loren.It transpired that she had just finished signing copies of her autobiography, "Sophia: Living and Loving" and in order to get away from the crowds, her press agent had arranged for a Rolls Royce to stop outside the shop so that she could effect a quick getaway.

＊　＊　＊　＊

Sunday lunchtime stag audiences are notorious for liking filthy humour but ironically, the most successful acts I ever saw were also the cleanest: Little and Large, The Krankies and Ronnie Cryer and his Marionettes – Ronnie was responsible for the biggest roar ever when the hump on his camel flipped open and a little man with a fez on his head popped out.

＊　＊　＊　＊

On New Year's Eve 1974 I did two comedy spots at the Strathallan Hotel in Birmingham. After ten minutes of my first act a man keeled over, everything stopped and in seconds he was pronounced dead on the spot. I then moved into the ballroom and ten minutes into my second act the world-famous snooker player Joe Davis, walked down the entire length of the room, taking five hundred pairs of eyes with him. By the time he reached his table *I was dead*.

* * * *

Mitch Revely, the singer, rang to say that he was in town and it was absolutely imperative that he saw me straight away. Jo explained that I was away. "OK but tell him it is extremely urgent and to stand by the telephone on Monday." (Up to then neither of us had ever heard of Mitch Revely). On that Monday, in the mid-seventies, I stood by the telephone. I am still standing there. If you ever read this, Mitch, the curiosity is killing me.

* * * *

A moment of high drama. A call came through from a very irate woman telling me that her daughter was pregnant and that she, her mother, was trying to trace the man responsible. She had stumbled across her daughter's diaries and the entry for 9th September 1977 described in lurid detail exactly how I had done the dastardly deed in the car park of La Reserve in Sutton Park. Whilst she was raving at me, I reached into my desk drawer and pulled out the diary for that year. On the exact date in question Shaw Taylor had me entertaining a room full of businessmen in Sardinia. I read her the entry, there was a long pause and then she mumbled, "Oh well, it must have been somebody else" and was gone.

* * * *

Charlie Lea told me that he had received a call from one of showbiz's biggest agents, Billy Marsh (who mainly handled artistes of the calibre of Morecambe and Wise) inviting him to his office the next morning. He arrived and was told, "One of my talent scouts saw your comedy act at the weekend. He was very impressed and we'd like to sign you up." Charlie said, "Mr Marsh, I've been with your agency for the last two years."

* * * *

Scouring the Internet I discovered someone offering a copy of our book, "Coventry: A Century of News", for £332.27 – it was currently available for £7.99! Oddly enough, it was *unsigned*. (A friend of mine said, after finding signed copies of my books everywhere, that the only ones of value would be those I had forgotten to sign.)

* * * *

Researching our book, "Memories of Walsall", Dennis Moore and I had been introduced to a lady called Betty Hodson who, we were told, had a wartime tale to tell and indeed, she had. In 1943 she was informed, by the authorities, that two young American servicemen were to be billeted with her. On the night of their expected arrival there was a total blackout so when they knocked on the door she had to let them into an unlit hall. When she did eventually put the light on, she found, standing there, Mickey Rooney and Bobby Breen – two of Hollywood's biggest stars.

* * * *

When Keith Price was researching into my mother's family tree he discovered a relative, Walter Pipe, who was fined £12, in 1631, for not turning up to be knighted.

* * * *

I was the co-speaker at a dinner, in Norwich, with the TV personality, Magnus Pyke. He was known for his extrovert and explosive windmill-like arm movements, as he explained various scientific experiments. Collecting him from the station, I found a miserable, taciturn little man who clutched his knees all the way to the hotel, without exchanging a word. When the time came to give his speech, he sprang to his feet, waving his arms around like a mad dervish, semaphoring to left and right (at one point almost knocking my head off in the process). On the way back to the station, we had the knee-clutching, silent version.

* * * *

My friend, the actor, Doel Luscombe, told me a similar story, Just after the war he was managing the little cinema/theatre on Guernsey. He booked Peter Lorre, by that time a very big star, for the unheard-of fee of £150, to make a personal appearance before the showing of one of his films. From the airport to the engagement the Hungarian screen villain grumbled and moaned endlessly. By the time they reached the venue Doel had just about had enough of him and deeply resented having committed so much of his very limited budget on this surly and ungrateful visitor. However, from the moment he walked on stage, although it was only a ten minute spot, Doel said it was all pure gold and the best £150 he had ever spent in his life.

* * * *

This happened to me on a train. Can you imagine sitting opposite a man who is speaking animatedly on his mobile and giving orders with an air of enormous authority – suddenly, mid-sentence, his mobile rings?

I was about to appear in concert with Al Jolson, Junior – a man purporting to be the famous singer's son. Unfortunately, he was revealed, as a phony, on a late-night radio programme and we both lost a booking.

* * * *

There are three unusual pictures in our home and they all have their own story:

1) Tony Mercer and I opened a garden fete at Weston-super-Mare, in 1970. Judging the art exhibition I was smitten with a montage comprised of cuttings from magazines. I assumed it was the work of a college student. The next day the artist arrived at my flat and turned out to be an elderly, white-haired lady who was thrilled that someone from the summer show wanted to buy her work.

2) Once a week, during that season, I did a late-night spot at Holimarine, in Burnham-on-Sea. On the night that I was due to finish the run the manager came up to me, "I'd love to book you for next week but being late in the season we won't have many visitors. I am afraid I can't afford to pay you," he said, "But I have noticed you looking at that painting of an Eastern street scene over there. Do one extra spot and the picture's yours."

3) I spotted, in the foyer of Bristol Old Vic, a painting done with a palette knife of two Harlequins gazing sadly at a rose held in the palm of one of their hands. Once again, falling in love on sight, I bought it, took it home and within 5 minutes of it being on our wall, Jefferson (the pop singer who lived in the flat above) offered me ten times the price I had paid.

* * * *

"JOTTINGS"

FIFTY ODD RANDOM DEFINITIONS

Abacus	–	something you can really count on.
Analogy	–	rear study.
Botox Treatment	–	stuffing your face.
Bumpkin	–	the act of striking a relative.
Car passengers	–	canned people.
Clothes	–	garments that man maketh that maketh the man.
Contortionist	–	someone with a different view of things.
Dinosaur	–	an aggrieved person in a restaurant.
Diverse Pursuits	–	pastimes enjoyed by underwater explorers, e.g. walking on the sea bed searching for ship-wrecks, blowing bubbles, etc.
Driving test	–	an attempt to get the L out of it.
Drunks	–	canned people (motto: "Absinthe makes the mind go yonder").
Eccentric	–	everyone else.
Elongate	–	a Northern expression of surprise, usually uttered in relation to an unusual hinged barrier or entrance.
Equator	–	someone who tries to be all things to all people.

Fascist	–	Scottish motoring champion.
Friend in need	–	the invisible man.
Gas/Electricity Bills	–	fuel's gold.
Graffiti	–	the writing is on the wall.
Helicopter	–	better understood if used in conjunction with, "He came home early and by —" (thus creating total ambiguity).
Hirsute	–	hair apparent.
Impale	–	to stick on the end of something (not as in "full stop").
Jogging	–	running fast in slow motion.
Kama Sutra	–	a book listing the various positions held by people in relation to one another.
Live and Let Live	–	what I always say.
Make-up	–	flaw covering.
Me	–	not you.
Modern Theatre	–	much a show about nothing.
Monosyllabic	–	using five syllables to denote one.
Monsoon	–	a Scottish youth.
Motorway	–	the shortest distance between two points with the most number of road repairs.
Music	–	a type of insect. The hills are alive with the sound of it.
Murphy's Law	–	the potato rules.

Normal	–	an eccentric's view of themself.
Over-Priced Commodity	–	the next object on the shopping list.
Pedagogue	–	a place for worshipping feet.
Party Whip	–	the scourge carried by Madame Zola as her contribution to the festivities.
Perfect Husband	–	someone else's.
Perfect Wife	–	anyone else's.
Picket	–	a striking example.
Quotation	–	a phrase, or saying, almost guaranteed to be misquoted.
Road Sweeper	–	a brush with authority.
Swimsuit	–	much-a-show about nothing.
Tattooist	–	someone with designs on your person.
Telepathy	–	follow my meaning?
Uttermost	–	a talkative person.
Violin	–	a hotel not recommended by the AA.
Waiting for Godot	–	the answer to the question, "What are you doing standing here?", put to a man carrying a placard which proclaims, "THE END OF THE WORLD IS NIGH". As he completes the answer a very large elephant stamps on his toe.
Xylophone	–	musical instrument, easier to play than to spell.
You	–	not me.
Zero	–	the word means nothing.

LOST FOR WORDS?

If a word's the wrong one for us
Open up Roget's Thesaurus.
If a word's misunderstood
Collins' Dictionary's good.

A MATTER OF TASTE

Some people say spinach
Has lots of good in each
Bite. I prefer broccoli,
Available loccoli.

HERE'S TO A LONG LIFE

Marriage works
If, like a Saint,
You say you're wrong
Each time you ain't.

SWITCH OFF

In secs my mind
Engages neutral
Confronted with
A prob computeral.

"CUSTOMS: ANCIENT AND MODERN"

During the research for my BBC TV quiz series, "Know Your Place", I came across several customs which were particularly intriguing. Here is just a small selection.

SNERT STUFFING

In the eighteenth century the indentures of apprentices in Yorkshire included the instruction that employers were forbidden to feed them more than four square meals a day. On the 18th April 1732, Milton Didlock, a mill-owner, fearing that one of his employees might starve to death, killed the youth, Helmut Snert, by force-feeding him a whole loaf. To this day, on the anniversary of Snert's demise, Northerners gather on street corners and uttering the ancient cry, "Sucks boo to thee, m'Lud", hurl slices of bread at any person seen carrying a copy of The Times.

THE TEWKESBURY THRASH

Takes place on Palm Saturday. A Medieval custom whereby husbands and wives confess publicly to any infidelities committed during the preceding twelve months. They are then paraded through the streets of the town and righteous bystanders belabour them with purple balloons, coupled with the centuries-old admonishment, "Oo's been at it then!" The number of miscreants taking part in recent years has increased to such an extent that they now far outnumber the onlookers. It has been suggested by ninety-two-year-old Cees Visser, himself a participant in the procession for the past twenty years, that the roles should now be reversed and the cry replaced by a loud yawn.

THE FLETCH FLICK

A craze reputed to have started as far back as 1973. Named after Wart Fletcher, a man with an affliction that would start as a gentle sideways rocking and culminate in a violent 'flick' from left to right. It is reported that on one occasion Fletch 'flicked' so ferociously he finished up with his head tucked inside the back of his trousers. People all over the UK, thinking it was a new kind of sport, tried to emulate his action.

The greatest exponent of the art of 'Fletch Flicking' was Chetwynd Plotnik, of Much Wenlock, who, by smearing the inside of his nostrils with a well-known adhesive, induced a spasm of truly awesome splendour, enabling him to clear a line of fifteen double-decker buses, concluding face downwards in a tub of lard. The latter expression, by the way, is not to be taken as a reference to Dora "Toll" Tole, of Butts Lane, Theddingworth, a woman of such gigantic proportions that people were charged 15p to walk round her. (The only exceptions were senior citizens and an army of local men known as "Toll Gropers", who were always made welcome.) Dora was referred to by most Leicestershire wives as that "tub of lard".

Incidentally, Wart Fletcher is credited with inventing The Ploughman's Breakfast, a meal that failed because it involved getting up so early.

AS SILLY AS IT GETS

The search continues to find this year's "Silliest Person In The UK". Emrys Bloemfeld had been short-listed until he was discovered lying face down in the newly painted gutter in Studley. He was charged with being drunk and disorderly and with having a yellow streak up his back.

KEG (or KECK or KEK) GLANCING

On the 15th April 1957, a steel erector, Alf Gulab Jaman, was detained by Birmingham police. He had been seen at 11.14a.m. kneeling on the pavement, his head in the gutter, peering up men's trouser legs. When questioned he said, "I heard the voice of God calling to me from a drain." The police released him after stating somewhat incoherently, through handkerchiefs stuffed in their mouths, that it was the best one they had heard in a month of Sundays. Later that day, however, he was arrested whilst standing on his head outside the Council Chambers. Once again, when questioned, he claimed to have heard God's voice speaking to him, this time from a dignitary's left turn-up. He was charged with committing an act of gross sexual perversion and trying to count the hairs on the Lord Mayor's knee.

This event precipitated a whole spate of similar incidents and hordes of men were often seen roaming the streets looking for men's trousers to look up. As the news spread the area became deserted and they then proceeded to look up each other's 'kegs'. This activity continued for the next thirty years, at the end of which the men returned home.

The originator of the pastime, meanwhile, was released from custody after promising to devote himself to charitable causes and to spend any spare time looking up his own trousers.

Although there have been sporadic instances of a similar nature reported in recent years it seems to have almost completely died out and Alf Gulab Jaman was last seen trying to persuade a chicken to take back a double-yolked egg. He was wearing a kilt at the time.

MAKING A SANDIBACK OF YOURSELF

No one seems to know exactly when this custom began but as long ago as the early sixteenth century, the women of Tamworth are reported to have been seen kissing strange men in public throughout the month of May. All this changed, however, in the mid nineteen sixties when Heathcote Coleman, a man who was so handsome he could only be viewed through thick gauze, came to live in Hopwas. Despite the fact that Heathcote spoke in a high sibilant fashion and was frequently seen in the company of older men with strange hairstyles, women found him irresistible. At any time of the year they would leap out from behind bushes and kiss him, not caring that he would immediately wipe his lips vigorously with the back of his hand and then spit. He finally made a formal complaint and magistrates ordered that forcible kissing should be outlawed for ever.

Despite recent attempts, by the committee of a local working men's club, to have the custom revived, the Tamworth councillors, including several older men with strange hairstyles, have always refused permission.

THE WHAT-IF-I-AM CEREMONY

Possibly the most mysterious custom of all, because no one has ever heard of it.

END GAME

Due to the success of their movement in America, following the commencement of prohibition in 1920, it was decided that there would be an Annual Mafia Games. In 1929, Deacon "No Nose" Quartz mowed down seventeen of the opposing team in just four seconds; a world record for the "Free-for-all". He was disqualified for jumping the gun.

DOWNING THE POLECAT

A Black Country ceremony dating back over five hundred years. Occurs at infrequent intervals and only then at the insistence of the local tourist board. (A word of caution : it is advisable that only persons of a strong disposition should continue – the publisher cannot be held responsible for fainting or other displays of overt exhibitionism.)

In Dudley High Street, at the stroke of noon on the third Saturday nearest to the last Tuesday after the second Wednesday prior to Michaelmas (or New Year's Eve, whichever comes first), a fire is ignited by rubbing together two elements of whatever. Then, using a recipe known only to the manager of Swinford's Video Varieties, Polecat Stew is prepared. It is rumoured that, traditionally, the basic ingredient has to be the Gornal Polecat, which is caught by whispering, "Here birdie, birdie. Here birdie, birdie," whilst squatting on a bystander's shoulders. The stew has such an effect on the breath that an ancient by-law decrees, "…that it shall only be fed to persons residing, or employed, at least ten miles beyond the town's boundaries." However, staff and customers alike maintain that local bank teller, Wesley Krampf, has managed to obtain a supply of the mixture and is using it as a mouth wash.

NOWT DAY

The most recent custom of all. In 1980, an Accrington councillor, Clayton le Moors, on consulting his desk diary, noticed that the 9th October was the only day in the British calendar that had not yet been designated as a Bank Holiday. He immediately called an emergency meeting of the council and insisted that this should be rectified. Despite cries from the Opposition benches, of, "Stop wastin' t' council's time yer big soft puddin'," he persisted, albeit unsuccessfully, with his demand. Since then, each year, the trade unions have called an all-out stoppage of work on the day in question. Nowt Day, being the only official working day left, is also known as, "The Most Boring Day of the Year".

RULES FOR LIVING

Don't break with tradition,
The die has been cast.
The key to the future
Must lie in the past.
So learn from the errors
That others have made
And follow their footsteps
Before they can fade.

Although if you ask me
The answers just got to be:
Forget all that nonsense
And win on the lottery.

ALTON'S BOOKS - STILL IN PRINT !

"I FORGOT TO TELL YOU"
"BIRMINGHAM: BACK TO THE FORTIES"
"THE BIRMINGHAM SCRAPBOOK Vol 1"
"THE BIRMINGHAM SCRAPBOOK Vol 2"
"BIRMINGHAM IN THE THIRTIES"
"BIRMINGHAM IN THE FORTIES"
"BIRMINGHAM: BACK TO THE FIFTIES"
"BIRMINGHAM IN THE FIFTIES Vol 1"
"BIRMINGHAM IN THE FIFTIES Vol 2"
"BIRMINGHAM: BACK TO THE SIXTIES"
"BIRMINGHAM IN THE SIXTIES Vol 1"
"BIRMINGHAM IN THE SIXTIES Vol 2"
"BIRMINGHAM: BACK TO THE SEVENTIES"
"BIRMINGHAM IN THE SEVENTIES"
"BIRMINGHAM: A LOOK BACK"
"BIRMINGHAM REMEMBERED"
"MEMORIES OF BIRMINGHAM"
"BIRMINGHAM AT PLAY"
"BIRMINGHAM SHOPS"
"BIRMINGHAM AT WORK"
"BIRMINGHAM: THE WAR YEARS"
"BIRMINGHAM AT WAR Vol 1"
"BIRMINGHAM AT WAR Vol 2"
"DOGS IN BIRMINGHAM"
"COVENTRY: A CENTURY OF NEWS"
"MEMORIES OF COVENTRY"
"COVENTRY AT WAR"
"MEMORIES OF STRATFORD-UPON-AVON"
"JOE RUSSELL'S SMETHWICK"
"MEMORIES OF THE BLACK COUNTRY"
"THE BLACK COUNTRY AT WAR"
"THE BLACK COUNTRY REMEMBERED"
"MEMORIES OF DUDLEY"
"MEMORIES OF WALSALL"
"MEMORIES OF WEST BROMWICH"
"A LOAD OF NONSENSE!"
"SHOCKING NONSENSE!"
"THE ORIGINAL ALTON DOUGLAS"

Contact leading booksellers or for **ORDER FORM** please write to:
Alton Douglas, c/o Brewin Books Ltd.,
Doric House, 56 Alcester Road, Studley, Warwickshire, B80 7LG.

www.altondouglas.co.uk